AND YET

BOOKS BY JOHN STEFFLER

POETRY

An Explanation of Yellow (1980)
The Grey Islands (1985, 2000)
The Wreckage of Play (1988)
That Night We Were Ravenous (1998)
Helix: New and Selected Poems (2002)
Lookout (2010)

FICTION

The Afterlife of George Cartwright (1992)
German Mills (2015)

NONFICTION

Forty-One Pages: On Poetry, Language, and Wilderness (2019)

AND YET

POEMS

JOHN STEFFLER

McCLELLAND & STEWART

Library and Archives Canada Cataloguing in Publication

Title: And yet / John Steffler.
Names: Steffler, John, 1947- author.
Description: Poems.
Identifiers: Canadiana (print) 20200185950 | Canadiana (ebook) 20200185969 |
    ISBN 9780771094521 (softcover) | ISBN 9780771094538 (EPUB)
Classification: LCC PS8587.T346 A83 2020 | DDC C811/.54—dc23

Published simultaneously in the United States of America by McClelland & Stewart, a division of Penguin Random House Canada Limited, a Penguin Random House Company

ISBN: 978-0-7710-9452-1
ebook ISBN: 978-0-7710-9453-8

Typeset in Jenson by M&S, Toronto
Book design: Emma Dolan
Cover image: page 315 *Handbook of birds of the western United States including the great plains, great basin, Pacific slope, and lower Rio Grande valley* (1908), The Library of Congress/ Internet Archive Book Images

Printed and bound in Canada

McClelland & Stewart,
a division of Penguin Random House Canada Limited,
a Penguin Random House Company
www.penguinrandomhouse.ca

1   2   3   4   5   24   23   22   21   20

Penguin
Random House
McCLELLAND & STEWART

For Susan Gillis
and in memory of Ken Livingstone

CONTENTS

AND YET

AND YET

You wrote at intervals from Madrid, Algiers,
Victoria and Corner Brook, and on a weekday
in June—a silk-wrapped chunk of Roman mosaic
deep in your duffel bag—you walk the old
dirt road to the valley's edge and see far below
in its fields, exactly as you remembered,
the house that made your journey a circle.
Your mother probably in the garden, your father
at his lathe. For years you've pictured them,
wanted to see them remembering you. Your
old self. You wait. You hover in the heat—
in the sight of the small glinting roof
you've longed for—still not ready to return.

SILPHIUM: A NOTEBOOK

We Make Our Long-Talked-About Trip to the One-Room School Museum

Sharp off the lake, the November wind we shoulder into feels
like 1953. The museum—a belfry, three tall windows along
the side—is it really my old school waiting down this street?
We're small again, all urges and don'ts.

The door thuds shut. Museum air. No schoolroom stress-fug.
No wet-boots-chalk-sweat-coal-smoke-stale-bread ghost.
"This used to be a Masonic lodge," the director says, leading
us to the cabinets. Rows of rulers and nibs. He shows Phil
an oleograph flipchart of the body's organs. Joanne talks with
his volunteers, three white-haired ladies pasting wildflowers
on greeting cards as they did in grade three. Past the labelled
erasers, I lean toward tacked-up photographs—

                                    a raw dirt
yard tilts glaring, humid under loud June trees. We're lined
up, backs to the hot school wall, squinting beside Miss Duncan,
who's acting happy and strange.
                          I hold still.
                               I'm not even picking
my knuckle warts. I'm watching the man poise his camera on its three
long legs. His smooth movements. I now know why Miss Duncan's
wearing a white blouse and brooch.
                        At my left, Wayne (horse-smell)
Brown elbows my ribs, his face a grey blur. At my right, Sandra Dooley's
warm placid arm (woodsmoke, pee).
                          The man ducks behind the black
accordion, its eye blinks like shears slicing a chunk of day.

If you sing before breakfast, you cry before lunch.
Lightning strikes the mocker.
Death slips in by the empty cupboard and cold stove.

> they want to land these children
> want somehow they don't
> know where their ache pulls at some
> far inside sickening they need to
> walk in plain *hello* not howl bare
> gutted what they felt is not real is not
> safe the side out here with you

In the mock-up classroom we sit at small desks. Phil says when
the local doctor came to their school to talk about health and asked
if there were any questions, Phil raised his hand and asked where tears
come from. The doctor beckoned him to the front of the room, took
down the photo of Queen Elizabeth and got Phil to look very closely
into the corner of the Queen's eye, where he could see the tiny little
hole where tears come out.

On the last day of school in June, I say, our teacher got us to bring
razor blades or knives or straight-edged shards of glass so we could
scrape our desk tops clean of the ink stains, initials and doodles we'd
left there during the year.

Joanne remembers the hatred she felt for her grade eight teacher. He
was so cruel, she says, her friend would throw up before class. And
then in December the teacher read *A Christmas Carol* to the class and
broke down crying, sitting there in front of them on a desk, a sight
that caused Joanne's hatred to open and show an unhappy human.
And as the man sobbed and read and sobbed Joanne watched the boy

in the desk nearest to him dipping the hem of the teacher's jacket into his inkwell and the ink soaking higher and higher up the flank of the miserable grey tweed.

a stack of blackboard slates leans against a wall, each
piece five feet square and more than half an inch thick,
their edges still bearing the marks of the stone saw's
teeth. They're for sale, and I want one. I want one of these
black rectangles still charged with the quarry where it was
cut, the nineteenth-century men carefully prying and rasping
it free, the horses that hauled it a hundred miles packed in
straw without breaking it, the carpenters who installed it
in some now-demolished school where generations
of words and numbers were smacked across it, the chalk
clacking, sometimes snapping or screeching leaving a white
scar, I want one of these smooth stone sheets to do what
with I don't know, it will just be me and a blackboard
slate in a white room with floor-to-ceiling windows
facing south

*

Gregory Curtis, *The Cave Painters*
Christine Desdemaines-Hugon, *Stepping-Stones*
Jean Clottes, *Cave Art*
Polly Fleury and Hope Kingsley, *Salt and Silver: Early Photography 1840-1860*
Götz Adriana, *Cezanne Paintings*
J. V. Wright, *Ontario Prehistory*
Max Raphael, *Prehistoric Cave Painting*
Nick Eyles, *Ontario Rocks*
Tomas Tranströmer, *Bright Scythe* (translated by Patty Crane)

*

SLIGHT BRIDGE

evening climbs Woodshed Hill's mauve
snow into its branches' grey haze, the foxlands,
the bearlands, the deepening turquoise west,

and here, a slim bridge made of watching, not
knowing, hangs between Woodshed Hill, closing
its dark door, and this darkening room

*

OLD FOREST

The walnut tables and bookcases had come down
through the family for generations. The children felt
their grandparents' lives lingered in the dark wood
and they understood who they were in the clock's
sound and the silvered light reflected into the living
room from the neighbouring slate roofs. But the war
brought that to an end. The bookcases and tables
stood naked for a while in a sidewalk market
and went somewhere else. The apartment's light
and smells and sounds, the dinners and piano lessons
lasted several years in the thoughts of the family's
last daughter. Her longing was the strongest force
she knew but it never touched what it reached for.
The loss of her mother's china, the weedy lot and
then the new building that stood where their green
front door had been mystified her. What had become
of her father's desk? Every house, every street and
walking person was a mark of grief. Hopes were
always the bud of pain's dark bloom. The world
was a plain under low rolling cloud, lustrous
as wet slate, dark as an old walnut desk.

*

Giacometti

the
brilliant
snow
field
the
sharp
north
wind
hide
behind
this
picture
of
them

*

New Moon

The words in both our books are wandering off
in constellations best investigated with closed eyes.
We click off the bedside lights. The rafters creak.

Ice grains trickle down the shingles overhead.

Somewhere in the room the cat rasps itself clean.

And then, a gnat-faint wailing my neck hairs hear
before my ear, a distant braid of suddenly swelling
screams—
              wolves are around the house,
                                          one shrill
yell my skin reads as a woman torn over the snow
in teeth—I strain to detect *Help!* or *No!*, set
to dart out and save someone,
                                          but the voice bursts its
human mask, streaking way beyond the orbit of any
self
into the yodel tornado.
                          We yank the curtains aside—

stars—fields' grey tarpaulin—forest's dark
bulk—

in the morning we'll look for tracks.

*

Giacometti

enough
clash
and
racket
without
your
hullabaloo
listen
...
...
windswept
snow
is
everything

*

BOARDWALK

To have a year-round path to the lake I build a boardwalk across the swamp.
The late winter ice is soft and grainy under the sharp sun but still holds me
    while I chop through it.
Black ooze smelling of beavers spurts from the holes as I pound in posts that
    will hold the boardwalk's stringers and slats.
Across the lake's ice, tiny geese and trumpeter swans float in shimmering layers.
And above where I work, in the silver maples' fine branches nearly dissolved
    in light, a white-throated sparrow sings in a moment that has lasted a
    million years.
I reach through a million years for the saw and cut a plank. There is no
    resistance to my arm.
A deer pauses—curious neck/ear slivers in the trees' slatted haze—and
    disappears.
I will soon be able to cross from shore to shore as easily as the sparrow's song.

＊

But when I go walking I want to forget everything I've read. The black walnut steps sideways, is not a history of itself or body of lore. It's a sound coming from all sides, its leaves are the smell you could call Atlantic or sentient or Cenozoic or music or walking to school.

*

PUSHING EVERYTHING ASIDE

Rising sun warms the pale cut ends of the wood
stacked in the lean-to on Woodshed Hill. All
winter the cat and mice, the jays and squirrels
have staged their plays on the elm chunks under
the wide up-tilted eave, and I've left their
theatre intact, burning thorn brush, worn-out
slippers, fish-fat-soaked magazines. I pay my
taxes at the long counter of the fisher's
tracks across the snow, and the fisher redraws
my acres' boundaries every night. Sometimes
I find them under the bed in a snarl it takes
all morning to undo. Sometimes I walk for
weeks back near the lake and can't recognize
anything. There are tents, smoke and voices,
white ribs high in the hemlocks. *I felt the swift
deepening of time.* Who set the beech tree here,
watching, watching, in its fine grey sleeves,
choosing not to say what it could? These
ladder marks where the bear climbed into cloud
and went to sleep. Or the trunk is occupied.
Someone in there on the phone. A mastodon for
godsake. How long has it been since a mastodon
called from here? Already red-winged blackbirds are
snatching the horizon line to weave their nests.

*

CROSSINGS

To get free of Nora, meowing us out of sleep from
the bedroom doorway, I grope down the dim stairs
following her swanky tail and open the door, letting
her dart onto the frosted porch—into the presence
of eight deer, clean as cream in the first light
on the field's brown snowless stubble. They lift
their faces to gaze at her as she walks toward them, tail
neither greeting nor hunting, as though lost in thought
on the way to the neighbours'—and sits, messageless,

not far from them. And the deer—straightbacked,
humpbacked, legs braced, bunchlegged, sideon, halfturned—
stretch their questioning necks and step toward her in
stops and increments, as curious as sheep, or pretending
to be, and Nora—nervous? what, her? nervous?—dawdles
briskly off to watch from amongst the bare forsythia
stems as, one by one, in their large space, the watching
deer gradually turn away, pulled into their forest trail
in slow leaps, until only one sleek deer grazing by itself

is left. It looks up, high-steps toward the forsythia and
stands in its growing aloneness, staring at Nora. Then,
raising its right front hoof, it bangs the ground, stabs
the ground again and again, as though commanding her

to flee or follow, and wheels, filling the sky with its wide
white tail, bucking its hind legs so high it disappears
in a somersault into the dark white spruce.

*

On the ground among bare rose canes
a robin is scuffling last year's leaves,
pausing, listening, cocking an eye.
Earthworms' tips are the first buds.

*

How could a weed be a book? (Aldo Leopold, *A Sand County Almanac*, p. 46)

*

SILPHIUM

Heads on Cyrene's bulgy lopsided coins might be Apollo
or Zeus-Ammon, tails is always a thick stalk of silphium
like a six-armed electric transmission tower or a triple-tiered
public fountain. What was silphium? It tasted like no other
plant. You closed your eyes and it went on up the palate,
fanning into new things, flavours and possibilities opening
each from each like a gustatory precursor of Bach's organ
fugues. Did it heal disease? Make the face lustrous
and young? It made Cyrene rich. Some think it was an
abortifacient. Was it incense? It couldn't be cultivated,
it would only grow wild. Was its smell exactly what people
mean by "what we want to be"? Hermes handed it to Orpheus.
It was worth its weight in gold, at night thieves killed the
guards and dug it up. Its seeds were the shape of Valentine
hearts. Will a silphium seed be found in some sandy Libyan
tomb, in the wrappings of a mummy or crumbling scroll,
a little heart-shaped seed we can water and nurture back
to life in our time and space? Its green cells held a nation
more ancient than ours. There were silphium cities, silphium
epics and lullabies. Silphium people gathered in markets
and councils, married and feasted and celebrated the beauty
of silphium life. They were communicating with beings in
other galaxies. Here we are, eating and inhaling every variety
of soot—barbed corkscrew molecules of ash boring into our
eyes and brains, growing cancers in every nook of our bodies.

For each creature we exterminate, we are evolving a new one
dependent on human flesh, their taxonomies strangely related to
deep-sea creatures, fungi, fruiting lianas. Signals are still coming
from Alpha Centauri: "Hello, Silphium! Are you there?" But
we cut it all down. We go around bashing each other with cars—
silphium is gone. It can't answer. We fawned on it, we
reached up its tall stalks like puppies trying to climb a kind
lady's leg. There it is on coins that last answered to human
desire twenty-two hundred years ago—if we don't include
what they bought for whoever sold them to the museum they
lie in now or the riches I'll get from making this poem. Nice
how we've always added value to the gold and silver of coins
with symbols of gods and monarchs and how monarchs have
attached themselves to whatever money can buy, so that Caesar
is there in my blood lusting me toward more life, toward new
shoes or a trip to Malta or a bottle of wine or an operation to
cut a sea cucumber out of my brain. I lie in bed looking up at
the ceilingless dark, longing for silphium. I read gardening
books, impatient with roses and carrots, longing for silphium.
I kneel, dribbling pinches of lettuce seed alongside the string
on the finely raked soil, my nose drips, my back aches, I rise
and dust off my knees and eat bread and soup and try not to
think of a world with silphium. Silphium would have made us
all happy with what we have.

*

Dear Green Thumb,

    Will the clematis eventually strangle me while I nap in the arbour? I love your column,

John

Dear John,

    Yes, it will.

Green Thumb

*

THIS IS ILLYRIA

for the rose bed: William Baffin
                  John Davis
                  Marie-Victorin
                  John Cabot
                  Henry Hudson

*

The lost landscape flickers briefly—bleached-out holes
and blurred names, Akerman, Hedford, Stevenson—the way
a dangled magnet flutters at a buried nail. You check the map
for the route to the Richmond Hill library where, in an hour,
we're going to read. Beyond the guardrail, the past lies
in layers, and I'm down there a few layers above Berczy,
under the factories and asphalt, sprawled on the farmhouse lawn
with Shawn, Carol and Tom, marvelling at the clouds' white
boil and the fine bottomless blue beyond the elms at the field's
edge. I couldn't then see myself streaking across the freeway-
framed horizon glancing down at us buried in July light.
What isn't a curtain that might part at any time?

＊

A Chair in a Thicket

the woods are slowly chewing—wide leafed-out
lips riding the jaws' relaxed roll as though munching
peanuts watching a game—and seem about to speak, lips
slightly parting, settling again, boughs dipping, lifting
in the speckled light, a walking pace, a thinking pace,
the strolling boughs speaking all the while, not
the boughs, the lips in the pollen-haze light, the shrilling
insects, the fine veins and eyes, in the listening,
the habitual intricate taking in, itself speech, selves
presenting themselves, forming skins, faces, shared
walls, building rooms within rooms, light-shuttered,
shade-lit, distant corridors, doorways, calls overlapping,
lapping into this cove, into this *this*, going elsewhere
still here, arriving new with no memory of here

Toolroom

My father is waiting for me to bring him a set of calipers.

The small room I'm standing in—the toolroom—off the back of the old summer kitchen, was once a pantry. It has a window facing west toward the barn. Its tall cupboard is full of electric motors, drill bits and pump gaskets. The wall-to-wall counter is piled with wrenches, cans of nails, work gloves, sharpening stones, coils of wire, boxes of bullets, a jar of mercury, a jar of DDT, engine oil, pulleys, fan belts, pliers, smudged folded packets of vegetable seeds.

My father is out in the barn crouched in the dim light beside the tractor handling the parts of its engine he's arranged on a piece of plank on the dirt floor.

I am motionless in the silence, in the window light, ranging my eyes over the crisscross curves and depths, the juts and nooks, the scythe blade angled down over the hardened paint brush under the monkey wrench and wooden mallet, the blue handle of a glass-cutter partly visible under that, the tip of a corroded plumb bob.

He needs the tractor to grade the lane, to scrape its half-mile length from end to end with a homemade drag, a kind of wooden raft with angle-iron blades on the bottom and a stone block on top for weight. I will sit on the block on the jolting drag, teeth rattling, field and sky like slatted blinds. He needs to fill the lane's potholes and level the hard mud ruts the Dooleys cut with their pickup in the spring, ignoring his *Keep Off* sign, tearing his barricade down to reach their house across the field once they'd churned their own lane to muck. But the tractor is broken.

Light in the toolroom is a fine, deeply silent grey. The rust-brown hammers, hinges, screwdrivers, funnels, oilcans, rivets, clamps, trowels, leg-hold traps are intensely motionless. Their stillness seems to contain centuries. To have gathered seasons of changing light and sound into mute knowledge. I will soon reach out and lift a chisel, a pitted bolt. I will hear the metal click and shift. I will remind myself of the shape of calipers.

My father needs the lane to be passable at least in summer to get things in from the highway and out to the highway that are too large and heavy to pull on a sleigh—a load of roofing tin, oats for the horse.

He is waiting for the calipers. They are not under the bucksaw blade. Not under the ball of twine.

He needs to be out of the city, the elbowing, the jeering, the taking what you can get. He needs to know that if the power goes out, we'll have lamps. If the stores are empty or burnt, the garden and chickens will keep us alive. He saw that in the '30s. He saw that in Germany in the war.

Not under the pry bar, the fence staples, the can of creosote. The silence is bottomless.

He needs the calipers to fix the tractor, the lane, the '30s, the war, the city, people's stupidity.

In the toolroom, nothing has moved for hundreds of years.

*

Late in the Day, Something Still Missing

a starling flock careens across
the cloud face like a ragged black
dog escaping from bees,
balks,
piles up into a tighter and tighter
lung and
coughs itself into a black plume hitting
a wind wall, warping
into a vortex, a tight-stemmed funnel
vanishing down some sky
drain
over the hill

*

Behind You

sometimes while waking up it's clear what the beads
slide on, you could say, "being human," but it's
nothing you own, not even things your parents'
parents told you, it's inside that, beyond the ears'
grasp—speak with a calm face to friends and
fellow workers while you're planning what to
pack, buy tickets in different names for different
destinations, only one of which you use,

whatever attracts you, go the other way, into
alleys into darkness into water into silence into
hardness into tightness into what falls through—
not "human", not "witness", not "logosphere", it's
what's still behind you when you turn around

*

Brackets

Among their raised three-pointed leaves, the viburnum
berries are yellow. They nod and shake a little in the warm
September breeze. Will the wild turkey come to pluck them
from the bare twigs when the ground is covered with
snow? Last year a solitary male stood here, wings tight
to his sides, stretching his long neck toward the small
frost-bruised fruit and launched his big body somehow
straight up on those kneeless stick legs, toes pointed
down as though imagining ballet. I picture this and write
the question down because the viburnum hangs over
the chair I'm lying in and I have time for a poetic thought.
Why is that poetic thought? In other places people's houses
burn with all their clothes and photographs, their children
die, men hold up rain-matted stuffed toys. Men with
rifles. Or cameras. Or notebooks. The wind rambles,
watery, stirring the rock elm's low-hanging boughs, and then
this page, and then the oak tree's boughs across the field.

ECLIPSE

The moon rises full through the pines
as the autumn crickets expect and
the stray cat comes calling and our cat
stalks it down the silvery lane, but
already our shadow—do we *have*
such a thing?—is creeping out
from its earth cave stalking the moon,
and by midnight only the barred owl
is calling, a dog nervously barks
across the cricketless field and the sky's
snuffed socket throbs out dark rays.

*

Night is full of passageways through which things disappear. Where they disappear to remains a mystery. Sometimes they seem to be standing just on the other side of the bookshelves and chairs. But the passageways move around unexpectedly. Handled by agents. Thieves of objects and lives. In the lawn a coyote opens a tunnel that swallows the cat—the cat that had more personality than the prime minister. And in the morning there's no sign of where that tunnel was or where the cat has gone.

*

Giacometti

the
moon
zero
in
brackets
stares
at
the
earth
love
being
made
and
unmade

*

CHARGED

Is there a law that makes us break
the law and take the punishment like a dog
hit by a car? I ache even among morning
glories and hummingbirds, suspecting I'm
charged without hope of acquittal, polarized
to repel every outcome I intend.

Or?

Can we join the clan of the dragonfly nymph
or hang the hypnotized pilot's portrait
at the head of the court or wear the icon
of mercury or the ash-covered ember or
swear by the twin signs of lichen and hail?

*

Woodshed Hill is losing its leaves. Those still clinging
swerve and tremble like a school of orange fish—
glittering—in the clear north wind.

Listen—again that *clunk* on the outside wall. Like something
trying to find a home for the winter.

Once in a while I think of the arrowhead I found years ago
and so far always find it again in some
box or drawer.

*

open doors all down the hallway, piles
of books and curtains, plates, shoes

I HAVEN'T LOOKED
AT THESE IN YEARS

I am watching us now, two dark specks in the white fields, my mother pulling me on a sleigh.

Even then, sixty-six years ago, I was watching—part of me already staying behind, watching us move on ahead out of sight, not sure if I was really seeing what I saw.

The vast cold sky is sharp as a spark, but the few barns and bare elms shrink away to the land's rim.

Her footsteps crunch the jagged snow, the sleigh jolting, swinging the sun side to side.

We are dashing from warmth to warmth, but my throat wants to go with the wind wherever it goes.

Her heels bounding ahead, my mother glows gigantic with struggle. Why isn't she sad?

We are specks, and the clouds of our breath fill the world. I stare at her red coat's swirling skirts like fireplace flames.

She turns and shows her smiling crooked front tooth. Why isn't she sad?

At the lane's end, by the white deserted road, she bends and brushes snow from the lid of a box. I stand looking over its edge as she opens it, snow spilling into its square wooden space where two frosted bottles of milk are waiting, their cardboard caps perched on short columns of frozen cream.

The bottles bundled beside me, we turn and begin the half mile back to the house where I'm already waiting, watching us come.

In the wind I am safe, naked as a crow.

There is barely space for us in the dark papered rooms. They are so full of old stains, so thick with silent watching. Why is my young mother hurrying here with such appetite?

THIN PATH

All evening the moon has coasted
out beyond the balcony.
                        You walk
the thin path across the gulf to ask
if there's anything it wants—a glass
of water, a shawl.
                        The moon smiles
and shakes its head, it's listening, it's
watching something you can't see.

You turn and walk carefully back
to where you were. For years
you didn't understand how deep
your shadow is and empty, how
it distances the things it falls on,

how it stretches out looking like
a path.

my beloved father was human, here's his hand holding
his knife, it's how I still remember him, I laid the knife
under his hand and covered him, my beloved sister
was human, mine were the last fingers to touch hers,
I placed this needle—it looks smaller here than it was—
between her finger and thumb, my father used to say
whatever eats leaves waste and hands are hungrier than
mouths, he said human hands are born toothless but
make their own teeth, here I am with my brush, and here
with the camera, beloved brush, the camera I'm not
so sure about, it meant a lot of arguing about catching
god, here you notice I've got it in both hands, very
human, and here I'm holding it in my teeth for a joke,
my father would have hated that, this pipe in my uncle's
mouth, see, my beloved uncle, was always a problem, only
animals carry with their mouths, my beloved father said,
leave the ashes, the scraps, the slash, the bones, we're
made to go forward, he said, that's why we haven't got
eyes in the backs of our heads or toes behind our heels,
here's my beloved aunt holding a pistol, my sickly cousin
with a book, some close-ups, hand with rosary, steering
wheel, telephone, cheese grater, matches, food dish,
beloved shoe, my father said never carry junk, remember
people only if you can describe their hands, them
touching you, some of them, hands want to reach for
what's clean, what's young, he said, what's past is
past, or maybe passed is passed, now, he said, is for
packing up, here he's shutting the trunk of the car

White-ceilinged space fills my face, which is the size of the room and includes everything in sight.

Recalling this, I know I'm on my back on a grey rug in the old farmhouse living room, but at the time I'm not aware of the rug, the room or my body as separate things.

An unstable presentation of light and shadow, warmth and coolness, surrounds me and shares my awareness. It materializes from a distance, swelling and full of purpose, then it falters, veers and fades. And then it grows again, at times feebly, partially, at times with sudden vehemence and force.

I take this activity of light and shadow to be a creature endowed with emotion and intent, a potent being like my mother or father but lacking human form. And although I witness its behaviour as unpredictable and independent of me, I also encompass it. It inhabits me. Its changes work my emotions and shape my physical presence.

The actions of this creature of coolness and warmth, doubt and resolve, its expressions, are never the same. It follows no pattern. It hesitates, it hovers between being here and somewhere else, it surges up, fully decided, glorious, powerful, bursting with plans for things to do, then its attention drifts away, no appetite, no confidence, leaving a queasy aimlessness, a vacancy which is also a kind of pleasure, like watching something fall out of reach, getting smaller and smaller, the shrinking aftermath of a sneeze, a spasm, goodbye saying hello, a wrinkled chill.

There goes its coming again and here comes its going away. And as it goes and comes I feel it slowly, very slowly lengthening out and sliding over me from right to left.

And then I realize what it is: sunlight broken by running clouds is passing through a tall south-facing window and casting a pattern of panes and sashes over me. (It was likely early spring.) I recognize the rug, my body, the window and that something in the sky is making the light strong and weak.

The flighty light-shadow creature has suddenly stiffened and gone into hiding in the window frame, in the floor, in my body, which now all seem set to stand their ground, mute, discrete and secretive, for as long as I live.

At the cutting board across from the wood stove
my mother unfolds the paper wrapper holding
a white-layered bacon slab and shears off
thongs of translucent rind she dangles for the cat

waiting beside me. The bacon pops and spits
in the black pan. The cat gnashes the rinds
with sharp gasps, jerking his head. My father
will go to work, my sister to school. I will

burrow back under the racket of newspapers
on the daybed or watch my grandmother root
through her rag bag choosing the next patch
for the quilt—a field of deep blue with silver

clouds, a field of brown furrows, a field
under cool green water. Or in my slow
coat and boots I'll follow the cat's black
whittled legs through the snowbanks' glare.

EVERYTHING'S ON THE MOVE

warm cool warm night-wind crazy with jailbreak,
laced with thawed swamp. spring peepers' shrill riot
oceaning over the porch, lifting my shirt. a halfmoon
staining the haze.

I brought these things up to bed—

and the three wild turkeys stilting halting over the lawn
at dusk, swivelling their blue Jurassic heads high
between bending pecks—

awake in the dark now, an ache in my scarred skull.

let all the unfrozen throats rant their blocked *pang! pang! pang!*

wind puffs the curtain from the sill and gasps it back—

sighs and clamour gathered from all down the continent,
calls across canyons, final farewells—here's all
my memories, all I ever wanted, all I loved and tried
to hold

the comet Draco sweeps the earth with its phosphorous
confetti tail—trickledown animism—detours, loops,
shortcuts—I drift through bedroom dark into the hayloft—
its prickly air—how close it always was!—dust-rich
light streaming through cracks and knotholes—heat
from the sun-stressed wall, the roof's creaking tin—I
lie with my ear to the tine-scarred floor, smell of old
pine—chaff—grist rubbed in the grain—waiting—wood
charged with the sun's hum—I hear you now climbing
the smoothed rungs—into the raftered heat, the sweetness
of dry grass—a loose plank rocks under your step—you
rustle, you kneel and lie beside me, don't you?—young
as before we were married—putting your mouth to mine

In winter, while we bent
over our workbooks in the rows of joined
desks, Miss Duncan would watch us
silently from the front of the room,
stationed
on the round iron grate where the cellar
coal furnace heat rose,
and her dress would swell like a silk
bell over her warmth-stroked
skin
and her gaze would surround me, mixed
with the murmuring dark algebra
of her perfume.

Ross Denby's words had brought me to the dark
dining room's window. January full moon.
The house cold, soundless. His words had wakened
me, drew me slowly past my parents' half-open
door and down the long invisible stairs.

The week before, while he and my father
jigged their lines through the opened ice,
he said, "You know this lake here's bottomless.
Bert Roddick took a team and wagon out to
about here to cut ice—broke through and was
never found." A mauve jackrabbit
darted in the twilight near us. Ross Denby
said, "Them hares dance under the winter
full moon." He looked at me. "You'll see them
dance, if you watch for them."

Beyond the glass, the prowlers' world stands
moonstruck, drained of dark. The swing
hangs from its pine bough, bone white. Its seat
I carved my name on casts a puzzle-piece-shaped
shadow sharp as ink.

My parents and sister are far away in a small
newspaper house.

In the moonyard, the knuckled black net spread
under the apple tree flutters. Blurs into moving
bodies. Red-spark eyes. A wisp of rabbits crouch
low flailing at mute drums. They burst apart, then
huddle, hunting for a lost ring.

They make a hopping carousel. They jig on hind
legs, wavering tall. They vault each other up
and up, white arch on arch to glitter-haze.

Behind my eyes a sun-filled plain. Open road.

Beyond the glass, under a frozen dome, ghosts
clamour toward the one bright hole—climbing
shadow rungs in the gaze of the great white owl.

MY FATHER TAUGHT HIMSELF ARC WELDING

Alone in the cellar he wired the welder directly
into the fuse panel's main feed, and every
evening billows of burnt-metal smoke pulsing
with green-blue light boiled from the open cellar
door next to the kitchen. *Zot-Zot-Zot!* He
was down there in gauntlets and dark-lensed
helmet, bent over the sparking rod while the lamps
and ceiling bulbs in the rest of the house wilted
to migraine brown, and *I Love Lucy* shrank
to a white dot on the TV screen. We
sat in the dark. The room, wracked by electric
fits, filled with vaporized steel. We could only
wait. He was under a spell, determined to master
the incendiary stitch that fused metal to metal,
and to waken him would have unleashed something
worse.

Little snow has made it down through the boughs
of the white pine and now the slope at its base catches
the winter sun. The fallen dry needles make a pocket
of hot rosin smells in the February air—a moment
you can occupy and pass through. When you were nine
you slept in this smell on warm pine needles behind
the school. An island washed in waves of glare.
Beyond the frozen marsh, the sun is sometimes engaged
in cloud, a breeze wanders here, handles the soft
surrounding boughs then strolls away ruffling a stand
of cedars. How little breeze it takes to make this pine's
high branches sing. Their faraway thin-brushed
whistle—braiding three minor keys—hungers—memories
of storms—fades—drops to an ear-touching whisper.

DISTURBANCE FROM AN EMPTY ROOM

My sister moved out at fifteen and the fighting
stopped and for months I heard my parents' footsteps
in separate parts of the house and the silence

of her room rang in my ears, I was ten, I spent days
alone in the barn's loft building a hay fort, a thick-walled
cave in the high cavernous space with its blades of dusty

light, in the stillness above the stall where her horse
had snorted and paced, where one fall Saturday afternoon
in my dark burrow, talking out loud to imagined people,

I pushed my hand out through a seam in the bale wall
to feel fresh air or imagined rain, and a hand
seized my hand, a dry cool flat-palmed barky strong

hand gripped my outthrust palm where I couldn't
see it and pulled it silently for a long time, I was
silent too, my shoulder and cheek drawn tight to the

stubble wall, and then the hand let go and I crawled
to the fort's low door and looked out not knowing
who or what I'd find, it was honour and the need to claim

sensible business that drew me out, and there was Barry
Knox, a boy a year ahead of me in school who had
never visited me before, I said, "Oh, hi," as though he'd

knocked and I'd opened the front door, and he seemed to have just awakened from sleepwalking with no better idea than I had of what he was doing there.

THAT WAS NOTHING

The elms have gone on their pilgrimage
in the grey wind, leaving no clue
to the routes they travel.
They might return with a passion
for awnings and deckchairs, but now,
the heat off, pipes drained, their rooms
stand open to snow and stars.

No, I never whispered any such thing

or cared

or had those thoughts you're thinking of.

I'm back in Newfoundland at a celebration of Al's
life and poetry. So many old friends. Smokey looks
as young as when I first met him. I'm so glad to see
him alive, I say, "Let me press you to my breast,"
playful and honest. I quote Ron Hynes: "It's all gone,
it won't come back no more," and realize I've come
unprepared, invisible, without really picturing the event
or its importance to me or the value my show of love
has for my friends. I should have brought a book
and planned to read a poem in Al's honour. I should
have written a poem. Al would have done that.
Celebrations and displays of love made the landscape
he lived in, whereas for me they often feel like
an accepted loss, consent rigged by those in control.
And yet what other presence do I have? I'll have to
ask someone to drive me to their house in the hope
of finding one of my books. In a room off the hallway
a group of gleefully furtive women are smoking hashish.
They beckon me in. I inhale from a small hot pipe wet
from their mouths, telling myself I'm crazy, I'll lose
track of time and never come up with a book, I'm farther
and farther from what I intend, I'm in *The Unconsoled*.

AUNT AGNES

I see in old photos that my Aunt Agnes
was beautiful when she was young—clear-faced,
endowed with an open future—the person whose dress
I thought was a kind of upholstery, who moved
like a pulpit on casters, whose hair was a layer of black
macaroni, whose small face was a pouch of old
accusations, who worked her mouth like she would
spit something when you weren't watching.

At the dining table we were nearly silent.

Uncle Walter breathed thickly through his nose. He could fix
radios although his fingers were stumpy.
"Would you like more cake?" my mother asked.
"No," he exhaled, "I'm full as a bull."
Aunt Agnes' eyes sagged at him, her throat swelled and coughed up
quietly, "Ach, Walter."

I blame you, Ontario, for her ruin and my squeamish ignorance.

She was still young when her twelve-year-old son was shot
and people went back to their jobs and dim parlours.

Simcoe's and Osgoode's and Russell's long-running charade.
If you haven't made a puppet to enter in your name, stay home.
And make sure that home is very small and no one else can get
in.

The man from Timiskaming or Nipissing asleep on the snow near the equestrian statue of Edward VII in Queen's Park. He had fallen off a bench. I paused to see if he was still breathing and walked on. What could I do?

SICK AND WRONG ABOUT MANY THINGS FOR A LONG TIME

Last night I wandered onto a small borderland road
and met my friend David Freeman who was witty and serene
about being dead, and today, after spending the morning
with Bly's Vallejo translations, groping through the Spanish
to see how his poems go, I eat lunch reading a review
of a book that mentions Edward Thomas hiking the countryside
to escape depression, so I go to see if I've got some Edward
Thomas on my shelves and find his *Selected Poems* with
an inscription in David Freeman's hand wishing me happy
birthday and adding in different ballpoint, "'As the Team's
Head-Brass' is one of the very best poems to have emerged
from WW1 (on p. 256)." Poor Edward Thomas who found
himself on the borders of sleep and gave in to the popular
logic that he could only prove his love for Britain's earth
by getting turned to worm shit in France. Which reminds me
why Lawrence was so great, refusing to sleepwalk into
death with his countrymen. And Vallejo, who knew
our dreams are not confined by sleep.

Ontario is sadder than landlocked Bolivia.
It has its Great Lakes, but they're cut down
the middle and, with American smokestacks along
the water's horizon venting brown fog, their shores
aren't thresholds to eternity. There are too many
fences and borders. If you can't walk through
a forest without thinking of fuel and intruders,
you're still indoors. And Hudson Bay, real
saltwater, is not in real Ontario, fortunately
for Hudson Bay. It lies north of the mirage line
where roads and travellers get refracted back
to Toronto or ripple and reappear up to their brows
in muskeg, covered in deerflies. Hudson Bay exists
in textbooks in the south and otherwise in its own un-
defined state. Ontario cannot go there to dip
its toes. It drives up and across and down and across
and up its concession road grid thinking there's got
to be some drink or pill or jackpot or old childhood
back lane or full-moon werewolf breakout to get
free of this private property asthma.

BRIDGE

The binoculars on the windowsill were for checking
the mailbox at the end of the lane. If the mailman
had turned it, there was mail.

Dressed for church, we bumped along the lane, all
of us elbow to elbow in the car, and came back far
apart in our thoughts.

I had to hurry over the bridge with my lunch bag
and books or I'd see the school bus pass the end
of the lane.

Through June, at the bridge, green plumes trailed
in the deep amber movement, minnows glinted
where Donna and I swam.

July starved the creek to a trickle—flies' noise,
stink, suckers gasping in glue. Ankle-deep
in mud, Donna said, "There's

nothing to do." Since spring her father had been
paralyzed, cursing in bed. She scooped a fistful
of clay and slowly

pressed crinkly grey ribbons out through her
knuckles—then pulled off her clothes, lay facedown,
twisting her long

bare body like an eel, easing and clenching
her legs until mud squeezed up through the backs
of her thighs. She turned

her smeared face up toward me and said, "Try it,
it's great." But I was not there, I was
already here.

Again I reach for the kitchen tap, forgetting the water's off. Since yesterday, filling the kettle from a jerrycan, heating water on the stove to do dishes, I've been reliving childhood routines.

On the farm our drinking water came from a hand pump in the yard near the clothesline. We brought it into the house in a pail that we placed in the cupboard under the kitchen sink. A white enamel dipper floated in the pail. There *was* running water in the kitchen and bathroom taps but that water came from a cistern in which all the farmhouse eavestrough downspouts converged. Leaves, twigs, bird droppings and shingle grit mixed in the cistern water made it unfit for drinking. And in droughts the cistern was always in danger of running dry. If it rained and the cistern was full we could flush the toilet more than once a day and live with something like modern ease. If it didn't rain we had to endure the shame of our dirt and smells and our father's angry rationing.

Most of the neighbours had drilled wells and modern plumbing. But my father had grown up without running water in the house, and he was sceptical about the pressure to modernize. He admired efficient tools but thought that domestic luxuries led to weakness and loss of character.

He couldn't drill a well and put in a water line by himself, and he hated hiring people. And the job would have been very expensive.

Habitual reminiscence is the skeleton of the mind, Freud said.

Our lives were shaped around water. In a dry summer, the sound of rain plunging through the downspouts into the cistern was like the sound of gushing cash. Sometimes, in a heavy storm, the downspouts would dislodge and I'd have to go out and fit them back in place while water surged from them. Laughing, drenched to the skin, wrestling the heavy live pipes, the thick foaming cascade thudding my arms and chest.

It was embarrassing when friends visited and couldn't understand our peculiar rules around the use of water and the reason for them. Why the tap water wasn't for drinking, why the toilet hadn't been flushed. It was easier to avoid having visitors.

The rules were beyond my control. They were an extension of my father's character and personal history and of his sense of cultural legacy, of how people should live on the land: modestly, frugally. The house and farm were an expression of his mind into which I had to fit. But the rules relating to water were also shaped, in part, by the weather, by rain and melting snow. My father's choices made us vulnerable and responsive to these conditions in crucial, fundamental ways. His rules and the rules of nature merged. Or he used the powers of nature to leverage his own power. That's how it seemed to me at the time. I felt increasingly helpless and isolated in our home with its archaic and unnecessary inconveniences, and from early adolescence I made careful plans to get away.

I've spent my life trying to sort out gratitude from blame.

There are many things I regret about those early years, but the way my life was shaped by the immediate natural world is not one of them.

Across the pale fields near the horizon a few hulks from the nineteenth century lie rotting.

Snow cover, cloud cover: one muffling cloth.

For hundreds of years people read and wrote in this light close to a window. Space between heartbeats. Where table and page hold still.

Depth reaching back to before ideas.

February is all the time in the world. A sea to be crossed in a well-stocked ship.

Books. Photo albums.

The caught look of distrust in my young mother's photo together with *The Enchanted Wanderer* will see me through the day.

In grade eight I was in love with the class beauties,
Phyllis Martin, Carol Fraser, Marilyn Roots. I slow-
danced with them under dim purple lights to the songs

of The Platters, holding their hot hands and cashmere
curves, breathing their shampoo in a nearly unwakeable
swoon. I was proud and lucky and took it for granted.

I barely noticed Hope Johnson and Beverly Croft, the pair
always strolling the schoolyard perimeter, watching things—
big Beverly, owlish glasses and ironic grin, and skinny

Hope, yakky flushed cheeks and pointy nose. They probably
loved books. So, when they strode up smiling stiffly and Hope
announced, "If you show us your wiener, we'll show you our

buns," I just kept walking toward the baseball diamond as though
they weren't there. Why do I think of this now? I don't believe
it's the missed erotic experience. I was a follower of James

Dean, and enough of my wishes came true. But I'm sorry
I couldn't match Hope and Beverly's brave stupidity. Already
naked, they called out my private cartoonish imaginings. But I

was zipped up in my 501s. What if I'd gone with them? Where?
The ravine? Would success and beauty have shunned me the rest
of my days? Or did they offer a chance to be actually human?

I stop. My arms loaded with wood in the hot dark corner
where the dog's dish is and the coats hang under the grey
plywood shelves my father made. Dark rubble of boots
and skates. My mother stirring a pan in the low-ceilinged
heat, the stove flickering red through its grate. I am seeing
all this from a distance. As passing. As soon gone. Myself
as well from a distance, spilling the barnboard chunks into
the battered bin, haunted by the pamphlet my father brought
back from the town hall meeting the night before, its cover
weirdly an aerial photo of our farm. A kind of newspaper
photo. Impersonal. Offhand. Our grey house with its dead
elms and collapsing barns crouched small and alone below
in the tilted grey fields. And superimposed on this dismissal
of us was an artist's conception of things to come—a red
four-lane highway cutting behind the barn, a green railway line
through the Hords' pasture to the north, a blueprint of building
lots and residential roads hovering like a net over the acres
where my father had planted small Christmas trees the mice
killed, chewing their bark off under the snow. I had not known
that my home was seen officially as a waste of space. I'm
thirteen, it's 1961, a place that I thought would last forever
is soon going to end. The woodbin, the warm dark air from
the stove is going to end. I am seeing my home from afar,
dissolving, and my parents moving into some unknowable
future, cut away from the only world I can picture them in.
As changed as I will be. What I'm made of—the stove,
the sleeping dog, the coats and flickering shadows—will be
gone. By an act of the township council. And my parents'

silence shows their acceptance. Expected loss of what they've
built. Already they've started leaving. This must be how they
felt in the war when my father was drafted. *Well, that's how
it is. No good fighting it.* I'd thought the hollowed wooden
treads of the stairs would be there forever, a path that vanished
people had worn, that I'd felt with my bare feet since I'd learned
to walk. I'd known I would leave these things years from now,
and the stairs would stay where they were. But now my bedroom
window, the well in the yard, the view of the southern hills—hills
I'm made of—will vanish. And in that strange new high orbit that
my mother and I share, looking down at the doomed stove, I say,
"We need a light in this corner," and she says, "Ach, he'll never
do that, there's so many things he never finished here." My
face goes cold. She has never criticized my father to me. Is
our house unfinished? It's what it is. The water bucket under
the sink is what it is. "He never sticks with anything," she says,
looking down with me at our small grey roof precariously far
below. Covering rooms where I've stopped bringing friends.
Snowed-in rooms swept by silence. I suddenly understand.
Swept by sadness. Myself a chance participant whose memory
reaches only to those stairs, the sash window's shadow grid,
the corner chimney's whirring nest of swifts. Fragments
my father has been building with. Following the blueprint
of his needs or Elmira's history or his sleepless strategies to be
safe. Far from the people wandering Germany's ruins. Far
from the home he lost in 1933. Six years at war. The arrowheads,
the black scraps of harness, the shards of flowered plates and
bones appeared where he chose to make a stand. Swept
out of sight again. The pan my mother is stirring, the stove I've
just fed, cancelled, falling away in the free unknown world.

NIGHTFALL

Across the field, half
merged in forest, two
deer have stopped, heads
raised,
          watching,
ears holding me,
their bodies the colour of falling dark,
darker
than the end-of-October field sinking
into night,
              one, turning
the way smoke turns in shifting air,
dissolves into
trees,
and a blurred patch opens, a third
deer slips
              from the air's grey
folds
where it was watching me.
the lit kitchen behind me.
dinner heating on the stove.

TWENTY-THREE

As long as I had a mind, I was thinking—I was twenty-three,
married that spring, my wife and I lying on the grass
behind the house where I'd grown up—as long as I had
pictures on my screen, I was thinking, I wouldn't care what
they were, they could be ragged claws scuttling, it wouldn't
matter, I wouldn't care, we lay on our backs on a blanket
in what I knew was the farm's last summer, earthmoving
machines were snorting diesel clouds just over the hill,
just over the hill rows of houses were going up, as long
as I was a witness, it wouldn't matter if I was one-eared,
poor, alone, I was twenty-three, my young wife and I
side by side on a blanket all that afternoon, watching
the light travel and slant and the light-soaked clouds build
and dissolve and build from nothing but fine, fine blue,
the moving, the moving-forward world, wearing and
tumbling, I thought, was what I was, I thought I'd always
be a kind of smile, a screen with the feel of a smile with
something filling it, I was wise, I was strong, I wasn't
afraid of what would come, there were years and years
ahead of us over the hills, sky and more sky, I thought,
as long as I had a mind it wouldn't matter what it held,
what it played over and over, I was invulnerable, I was
twenty-three, I knew that awareness and victory are
the same thing, the world is all story, it can't help being
story, and whatever that story would be would be mine.

WINDOW

Maybe my legs had been hurting again. In the dark
sleeping house my father propped me on the back
of the sofa facing the tall window. He said, "Look

at the moon." Its cold blazing whiteness filled
the sky above the pine's snow-laden boughs and
dissolved my pain. Dissolved my small body,

my age and name. And beside me my father
was no older than me. The shared moon clearly
filled our witnessing the way it filled the sky.

at the edge of the fields on the edge of Elmira, my mother
is travelling farther and farther into her past. fields usually
snowy stubble when I pass through. in her last days
she was back before I was born, had never imagined me.
cloud-grey space with distant barns. back before she
was married. beyond the huddled smokestacks and steeples.
her father with his gold-braid cap in the town band. wide,
wide silence. crows. the swelling and dwindling *wwhoosh*
of a car on Highway 86. had just written her grade thirteen
final exams, Latin, History, five years against what her
father wanted. her teachers shaming him to let her stay.
at eight o'clock and four, the Great West's whistle still
shrills over the frozen stubble. trees hear it in the hairs
of their roots. in the shaken machinery racket again
she swerves her hands, swerves her hands past the fast
blades carving boot welts from bins of felt blanks. miles
out in the dusk the small thin howl fading away. the town
in its faint luminous veil. down the belt-driven row
her foreman father hunched working a stitcher. wind,
rainclouds, sun. leaves uncrouch in the oaks' bent arms.
rain and sun. a man drives a mower past the tilting
stones. felt-dust in her throat, itch-swollen eyes. Opa
and Oma Hoelscher came from Grebenau for something
good. everything in a wooden trunk. wind and snow.
the boarder upstairs calling, *Dodie, bringen mehr heisses
wasser!* two bone buttons left in a dresser drawer smelling
of liniment. she never went on a journey alone before.

PAINTED CAVE

DARK STEPS

I remember these steps going down and
down, darkness sinking away,
the flickering lamp.

I remember this passage to the right, its cold
earth-smelling draft.

In there long ago I sang with my parents, ashamed
of my random erections, mouthing shared words, watching
the grownups' faces—men and women helpless, eyes
closed—singing.

In there for years I worked on an image
while my first wife and children went away. That one,
I think, that someone has reworked.

What did I mean by the bird-headed man pierced
by spears?

This is all my lost mind.

The crags, the beauty spots and scars that
might tell us Woodshed Hill's age and old
employment are hidden under a white cast
with only small holes for feeding tubes

and air. Maybe Woodshed Hill's not there.
Maybe its February dreams are actual travel
and it's down south or back in the Pleistocene
or visiting family in Alpha Centauri. Nearly

invisible in the morning glare, the forked
walnut whip I planted three years ago cracks
the snow slope with its sharp hairline
shadow. The mechanic's explanations never

snap the question chain, never make the asker
an actor. Walnut buds, wren chicks will soon
turn this cold case inside out and use
its lining for clothes.

FAR FROM TOOLS

the poem wants
its clothes, it is so thin
it shivers invisible
in the mirror in the cold
room, it cannot
tell itself from the reflected
bookshelves, the bit
of window showing cloud,
snow, it wants to be something
other than invisible-
wanting-to-be-something-other,
its mirrored absence
is a pain it has difficulty
accepting, difficulty
seeing as clothes, okay,
it knows the window,
the snow are clothes but
it's sick of them,
it would love to see an iguana
turning to face it,
iguana eyes looking deep
into its own, its lips
opening chalky jade-grey
lumps and points like
talking lichen

The guide's house is hard to see.
Its roof and low walls are built
of the birch and maple growing
around it. From his morning fire
smoke still drifts from the chimney
into the April air. There are no
windows I can see and no possessions
lying outside, not even a bucket
or axe. His living room must be
the forest. I imagine him going
into the house to sleep or wait
out a storm or sit in a different
darkness. I wish I could live in
the guide's house without feeling
lost or lonely or needing to lay
walkway stones. I wish
I lived in that birch-filtered light
with things as they are, not
thinking their names.

"Why does the chickadee's delight in sunflower seeds never diminish?"

"Because, as it passes from the chickadee's beak to its stomach, the sunflower seed acts as the chickadee's brain."

"Right. And the sunflower?"

"The sunflower is delighted to go on a short trip, knowing it will soon be planted again."

"Very good. Okay, now, why is the sunflower delighted by the sun?"

"Is it because the sun pours out the concentrated sweetness of vowels and the sunflower is a structure of dry fibrous consonants?"

"No."

"Is it because the sun is immortal, famous, and has thick shining hair?"

"No."

"Well, is it because the sunflower thinks the sky is a mirror and the sun a reflection of itself?"

"No."

"Okay, why then *is* the sunflower delighted by the sun?"

"Because the sun's delight in chickadees never diminishes."

"Is that logical?"

"What are you going to dream about tonight?"

A RANGE OF HILLS

Bears lug Woodshed Hill's bulky darkness into their
dens. It wakes up with them, famished, itchy with buds.

Deer whisk its moonlit branches across highways
in front of cars. Fishers ransack its theatre, littering

Pine Valley with the actors' heads. Coyotes lope
away, clutching the hill's money in their eyes. Jays

slash holes in its canopy—their cries disperse its
last leaves. A fox walks across a little fresh snow.

Waking up, I see its tracks disappear. Woodshed Hill
is there in the window. And in the pages on my desk.

Early March sun hot on the coffee table and my stocking feet, I'm
looking at photos of iron oxide and charcoal paintings someone made
in near-darkness on the walls of Chauvet Cave near the Rhône River
32,000 years ago. Minus ten degrees Celsius outside, but the light
swells on the snowy yard before flooding the window. Jean Clottes'
book *Cave Art* open on my lap. It's strangely easy to think in
thousands of years. For 25,000 years we told the same stories,
engaged with the same gods, the great animal rivers, the obdurate alien
fellows, stacked up dense and barging, rhinos, lions, bears, bison,
aurochs, mammoths, in the tundra's slopes and valleys, never far from
ice. For 25,000 years. Used the same kitchen utensils, answered our
children's questions with the same words. The herds of thick-bellied
horses, the reindeer, red deer, ibex flowing north and south, upland
and downland, always pursued by the poor sun. We watched and
adored them, filling ourselves like ticks with a drop of their vast
life. We were sticks, we were zigzags, we were eyes only, drinking in,
swallowing images to build ourselves, lines and words to hold the
animals inside our limbs. No stars or sun. The reindeer were the sun.
No plants or rivers. The horses were the plants and rivers. No human
faces. Only animals. We were invisible. Bottomless. Witnesses.
And when the ice began to melt and forests crowded the tundra plains,
some of us followed what was left of the deer and the ice northeast
into America, to Perth, where I sit with photos of Chauvet Cave, and
some of us stayed in the warming forests and raised sheep, pigs and
wheat, made carts and explosions and portraits of ourselves as the sun,
and soon sailed west here to Perth, where we didn't recognize our
cousins from only a few thousand years ago, had forgotten all our
shared stories, our old gods, except in sorrowful turbulent dreams.

That small breath jolted out seeing clouds and
land suddenly gathered into bison or deer,
shining in them—*aahhh!* An adoration gasp.
Pleasure returned to the pleasure-givers
in gratitude. A caress reaching out from
under the larynx—this was so well understood,
it had its own word, as one might say "a laugh,"
"a shudder." We don't know how the word
sounded, but there are many carvings of it,
of the creatures that caused the sensation
the much-loved word described. Carvings
in bone and ivory. Also paintings on rock,
and a few models in clay.

WINTER QUARTERS

from the goatpath ledge over the frozen river,
with paints, scraper and brush in a bag on my back, shielding
a lamp,
I wriggle into the mountain

inside is the heart's sky

what am I? a sign for hunger. sticks held together by bawling
or jokes

my bared hand burrows under her coat's cold leather

beyond daylight, beyond wind, beyond the slither-escape you touch in
slit bellies—nose and ears find the deer's passageway, the route summer
takes to her winter quarters, across plains and plateaus, over glaciers
and passes, down into a valley where the sun lives,
where bison are born

flame-light staggering under the shoulders' onroll, the dark animal-
honey flecked with gold eye-glints pours through my paint-stained
hands, taking the black-manganese and red-ochre flesh I offer them

daubing ankles and lips, I sop their heat into my starving
space

and because animate matter always has at its core
a soft quick, and brains and hearts need to be nearly
mush, the great currencies have all been versions
of flint. (Even the earth favours gladiators over
poets, limestone makes its bullion from thick
skulls and teeth, only once in a lucky while we find
fossils of flowers or tongues.) But those pure

hard tools for cutting and smashing survive the millennia
still clearly describing their vanished opposite,
the hot flowering beauty their makers fed and defended.
I claim this, that all the axes, spears, arrows,
swords and daggers were for guarding tender life, not
ripping it. I claim this. I claim this. I claim this. Shut up.
I claim this claim this claim this claim this claim this claim this

WALLS

Through the damp whispering draft, through
my ringing ear and the echoed *plink, plink*
of a distant waterdrop, I hear the people's faint
blended voices seep through the cavern's walls.
They are talking or singing in a neighbouring
chamber, their voices close but blurred through
thousands of years. I think they are here to
honour the animals' birthplace in the earth's
night. I hear them come closer. Just on the
other side, they reach toward me brushes
dipped in ochre and black manganese and
paint my shape on the thin surface between us.

If language has learned to live in the mind
the way racoons have learned to live in the city,
maybe words can go feral again, smother in vines
the sign saying *City Limits* and make me
dream when I think I'm awake.

                          Come on, trees,
I'm waiting to take dictation!

I have no idea what you're going to say
or if it will sound anything like birdsong or boulders.

Boulders?

        Fewer and fewer things fit
in my hands. Something the size of a steer or small
car is brushing the backside of whatever I'm
seeing and hearing—
                    like that huge
carp I once felt sliding against my
hand in the cold muddy water I reached down
into until my ear and cheek lay
under the surface

What man with a framed licence and a ring engraved with a compass and ruler
has laid out the boundary lines of the oak's estate? Its *soma*, its *miyaw*. In what
charter is the border between *bark* and *aer*, *ojiibik* and *aki*, *wrot* and *erd* set
down? The oak spreads into the streaming light *phos*, *giisis* and climbs
the condensed code right to the sun's brink, it's that tall, swims up a radiant
sugar cascade millions of miles high, the sky *pneuma*, *lyft* streams through
the oak's pores, pours through the tunnels and galleries *waanzh*, *bloma*, *miskwi*
the street map, metro and hallways of Mexico City and all its traffic are simple
and small compared to this oak grown into the wind, into the suburbs of air, the
commerce of breaths and whistles *kreas*, *carnem*, *wiiyass* carbon and oxygen
bales, tanks, pouches, veins and aerial alleys, wrens' routes beyond the ken of
London cabbies *widu*, *xylo*, *mitig*, *wod*, *vates* while roots drink from the heavy
dark, the depths under old words, sleep *gast*, *manidoo* the roots are not afraid
to enter every room, every thought you have, your dreams and faint
     rememberings,
drinking the knowledge into its growing reach *gikendaasowin*, *manas*, *munih*,
mantis you would never explore this one oak's forest if you had all the lifetimes
from Lascaux to Mark Rothko. And the light? Who has measured out its
     border
with the sun, counted the eyes it employs, the forms it paints on nothing? Who
has set the sun on one side and the sky on another? And the water, the earth,
the heartwood and me *heorte*, *giiyoon*, *gaia*, *erd*—my looking and being here—
who has put a percentage to each of them? To the heartwood in me and to me
in the oak's roots? *treo*, *truce*, *truth*, *bimaadan*, *zhiibine*, *du*, *duer*, *endure*.

Put your boots on backwards, pull your shorts down over your
eyes and let's go over what you've heard and said so far today.
Under the radio's rope bridge, under the news site's catwalk
grate, the gorge's torrent's noise, treetop mist—you were here
at four in the morning, your hands empty and nothing that showed
in a mirror but your clear-hole eyes, your mouth time-lapse
talking in reverse, back through childhood, through parents'
parents' cracked pale sloped thin muttering lips showing
more lips underneath, mouths inside mouths saying "world"
"wild" "wald," back through the plush-lined gulletry, earth-
tunnel-breath—all those long-dead selves are still thinking
you. Clear-headed. Your world is what they see. Your eyes
turned this way and that by a girl with red paint, two quail
eggs and lamp, about to go into the darkness of Pech Merle.
Er, ter, der, de, da, met, meter, mater. To be able to break all
the furniture, axe down doors and walls, burn the roof, roll
around outside with ants and asteroids and still leave a trail
of words you can pocket one by one all the way to your front
door—is its paint more weathered than you recall? Your chair
thicker, heavier? Dinner does taste of some stranger's touch.

WHAT KIND OF TRACKS ARE THESE?

This morning, is the interrogative the only working gear?

Could we say it's similar to reverse because operating in
Why? or *How?* we can't clearly see where we're going or
gain much speed?

And don't we find ourselves slowly reviewing a landscape
we earlier passed through taking it in only subliminally if
at all?

And aren't we now seeing the backside of what we took for
the front?

Is it stupid to assume that the first glimpse we have of a thing
is its front?

Does looking back at the way you've come make you realize
you're lost?

Which European philosopher believed that asking questions
delays or deflects the movement of time?

Are you irritated by lists?

If you could swivel your head like an owl would reverse be
equal to forward?

Likewise, if we refuse to accumulate answers, can a barrage of questions offer vertical lift?

Are questions inherently more comical than statements?

While a question clearly leads to a gulf that anyone might fill, is it not true that statements use their bulk or authority or menace or brutality or beauty or their intimidating confidence or blurred complexity to conceal the empty gulf behind where they started?

Do you assume there's someone inside you who could explain how you got where you are?

CAGES

Back and front I'm slung with empty
cages for wild birds. House wrens,
brown thrashers. Their long
various songs and abrupt certainties
are all around. I catch them
and take them away with me,
spelling each detail out until it's gone.

Reading Susan Howe's thoughts on the writing of Hannah
Edwards Wetmore, I have the impression she's patronizing
the eighteenth-century woman ever so slightly, moved but also
charmed and a bit amused by her quaint naivety—that
American notion that people from earlier eras were a bit
simple and laughable, apt to be more histrionic and earnest,
lacking in irony—and I build a case in my mind: how
because people *were* more exposed to hardship and death
in the past, living on closer terms with the slaughterhouse,
the workhouse, slavery, facing the stark consequences
of poverty, accident and isolation, without our medicines
and securities, it was natural for them to express their
struggle against darkness and annihilation with extravagant
drama, and while this might make them look like morbid
fire-and-brimstone yokels to some of us, it's really we
who are naive; our technological comforts have pushed
catastrophes a little farther into the background or future,
but since we're still mortal and since it's not clear how
long our sheltering culture can last, at some point we'll
need to deal with some form of famine and plague. And
yet, on going back over the pages of *That This*, I can't find
any place where Susan Howe patronizes Hannah Edwards
Wetmore.

I paint my face white because I run a small theatre
where you can watch things disappear. I paint
my nose red because I'm always crying and often
drink from a pocket flask. And I have a cold or am
allergic to something. The crown of my stovepipe
hat, wreathed in black crepe, is broken, but I let it
flap. It is my childhood beating its breast, and if
people laugh, that's the whip on my back I count on.
Hasn't a bigshot's violent hatred always been
the law? Even up close everyone's far away. On
the balcony I'm sarcastic as an old-fashioned crow
although the building teeters. I've cut words from
books and posters and taped them all over my patchy
suit. You can start reading my sleeve or collar or
crotch, it makes no difference. I tromp around
bowed down like Sherlock Holmes with a huge
magnifying glass, absorbed in my tracks.

In the late autumn, in the afternoon as the woods start
to darken, the triceratops comes down the rocky slope
northwest of the house and crosses the field. I watch

from the kitchen window. The setting sun or pale dying
light is always at its back as it ambles east, hoisting
its weight with a little skip and light rhythmic step,

the way elephants do. There's somewhere it wants to
spend the night. Or it walks and naps—one way or other
it follows a circle that will bring it back to the crest

of the ridge tomorrow at exactly the same time. I could
follow its tracks to find where it goes, but I only think
of this now. At the time, I always gaze at it without

attempting a thought, as you might gaze at a lake or
trunk of toys. Its hide is stiff-plated and coarsely
pebbled in glossy greens and rust-browns. When it

swings its beaked three-horned head toward me it seems
to be reaching in through the window the way you
grope through the coats in a closet looking for keys. Its

eyes shine phosphorescent green like the galley portholes
I once passed at night on the deck of the Newfoundland
ferry out in the Gulf of St. Lawrence in fog. The cooks

were inside in the small room's steamy light, bursting
out of their white unbuttoned jackets, smoking, mouthing
words, gesturing bare-armed, drinking bottles of beer.

The call is some poor prisoner reciting
hello she's with something
something research outfit doing a survey
on shopping habits. I set the phone
down on the sofa, continue on
to the kitchen to cut another piece
of Manchego cheese, oily and slightly crystalline
in its structure, hang up the phone on the way
back to my reading chair and munch
the cheese slowly with sips of red wine. Nothing
is blocking the path, but I know
what it is
and hit it with my stick, making the two wrestlers
break their hold on each other, and they
stand there, *no*
on one side, *thing* on the other,
as plain and naked as can be, and I walk
on between them, surprisingly
happy in spite of the mid-April cold
and being alone.

MUSÉE DES BEAUX-ARTS

A box of family keepsakes you can walk through.

"Tour the Western Tradition," the brochure says. "Start
in the Late Middle Ages on the fourth floor and descend
through the centuries." Contemporary galleries
are in the basement.
                              The elevator shuts out the foyer's
noise and ascends into the roots of the upended tree.
Why do I expect vestiges to be gruesome? The toys
and brittle books our parents treasured as children
always seem grim. Poor. The chipped tin horse,
the paralyzed doll serving the same dark imperative
as those carved African heads studded with nails.
                                                    Alone,
I follow the hall into a dim room with rows of clear spot-lit
cases, portholes into the deep brain, each housing
a painting on gold worm-holed wood. Altarpiece
parts. The altars, the damp murmuring churches and smoky
lanes all cleared away.
                              Each painting worries over the same
scene: hunched brutes nailing an intelligent young man to a thick
wooden T. Mallet blows. Blood. Spiked hands and feet.
The pain-wrecked man's upward gaze.
                                        It's hard to be human.
The mind a curse, since we're made to rot. Slaves to our guts
and crotches. Killing and mauling. Why attach *ergo sum* to this
crap? Spike the brainy bastard down! We're all spiked down.

Kill him and get back to being happy as larks, happy as pigs
in shit, happy as morons with mallets.

But the next room's gilt
panels show a young woman holding a child on her knee. Through
the glass her serene joy glows.

Her child's joy glows.

OLD WORLD

　　for Stan Dragland

Along the trails in the camps every day some were born.
Their mothers nursed them in plundered farmsteads watching
the buildings burn before moving on, the owners
twisting in nooses from trees. In log-walled shelters
their mothers wrapped them in kisses and charms, rocked them
all through the fire-lit telling of raids. And as they learned
to braid fingerbones in their hair and make axes gleam,
younger brothers and sisters were already following them,
sharing their awe at the bearded heads their uncles
nailed to ridgepoles and wagon rails. For each
lost to the calling of blades and mauls, for each one
lying watching flies pulling their legs
free from his blackening blood there were five
of his kind striding to take his place, riding out, sailing
out to harvest what others treasured—blood, gold, horses,
slaves, houses, fields—no wonder a few
dreamed of a quiet garden filling all their needs
and wore on their necks carved ivory tablets showing
a hand reaching down, pulling a naked human
headfirst up through its split scalp,
　　　　　　　　　　　letting its old skin clothing fall.

CELL (THE LAST CLIMB)

for Louise Bourgeois

It must be true, the flustered mind—the still famished,
homesick mind—is finally drawn to a cage—or—all along
the cell we've lived in was open—its bars are branches
and its trellised gate leads to the foot of a spiral stair—old
clanging treads familiar from precarious nightmares or
a workplace—where sometimes one floor down you glimpsed
your younger self lost in its wishes and maps—but now
the steps rise to an open roof among clear blue spheres—like
you'd hang above a crib—a riddle to explain space—Atlas
has escaped there, leaving—sunk on the floor the pair of massive
cracked wood balls she lugged all her lifetime—you've
escaped and left your nerves' sensations trailing—spooled
from the Old World tapestry you tried to mend—red
from its butchered parts—in the stairway's space your threads
are gathered to a high-peaked tent as though by flying
birds—maybe—maybe we can't know what we say and
make, and why, until we've gone where nothing is yet visible.

TREES AT SAINT-RÉMY

the air is burning and turning to earth

or the earth's mind is pouring out

green bolts dart between earth and sky, sky and earth so fast they

print themselves on the eye and seem to be standing still

remnants of blind ancient urgency flying past

even the smallest plum tree grabs the sky and waves it like a flag

it doesn't matter what's gorging on what, just seeing the turmoil is
a shot of god, but it's hard not to regret the knowledge-scald, your
self bleached away, worn poor, mute

lonely

when you mention the noise, people step back inside, their faces
slam shut

*

the noise a burning city makes—if you were to paint that

Herakleitos wrote: "Everything becomes fire, and from fire
everything is born" the young almond in late February

shoots green wires into your eyes, breeching the nerves' filter
caps, ramming lit gas down the spine, snarling your

boiling your

giving your thighbone marrow that orgasm ache

shearing your puppet strings—throat going *unh! unh!*—banging
up through the neck, exploding the brain

*

human nature likes to hide in the hope of longevity, how many
crows in a wheat field can we take?

*

a permanent bruise on the back of the eye

a thin curtain easily blown away

THE SEA STILL LOOKS WELCOMING

a small glowing corpse cocooned in pale
turquoise wrappings

I carried it up to the rocky pasture,
it weighed no more than a willow basket

April wind blew through the stones
of the hut where I laid it

scatters of light and rain will feed it,
birdsong and blown snow

letting my hands swing, hungry, I walk
down toward the village, red in the evening

EXCHANGE

The ancient Celtic warriors (or
admirers of warriors) spoke their pledges before witnesses
on the brink of a bog, making their vows famous and irrevocable by
throwing a lightning-alloy sword worth more than a man's life
into the black muck,

or
they were delivering treasures to their dead ancestors, thereby
obligating the dead to lobby on their behalf with the gods
with whom their dead mingled in back of the changing
clouds and hills,

and so
they threw their gorgeous bronze blades—images of their souls—
into the bottomless fens,
the black liquid night into which their ancestors and all the past
had vanished,

and we,
trowelling peat, reach out and catch their votive treasures
like tossed bouquets,
and leaning over museum cases, see their swords within our
reflected faces.

An excuse to poke through Rideau Antiques—could we find
a cayenne shaker like your small china parakeet?

In an aisle of glints and tarnish I knelt peering into a low
cabinet's darkness where a brown-orange rabbit sat, downcast,
trim, among blowsy cartoon figurines. I snaked my fingers
in and lifted him.

Seven holes in his lowered brow, under his paws a tiny
cork. Probably '40s Japanese.

For thousands of years he's been travelling through Thessaly,
Capodimonte, Meissen, Sumida, exiled from the ancient world—
pensive, one long ear fallen back on his shoulder, one askew—
oblivious to who was moulding and painting him.

Our table where he now sits filled with cayenne is no more
memorable to him than the auctions and junkshops.

Once in shadowless midday he kicked the whole planet away,
blurred mountains faster than any wolf, laughed, gallant,
savoured every petal and frond without needing to hunt, and
pushed hip-deep into honey's honey over and over—it was all
waves of gold smoulder up to the roots of his teeth and then it was

getting dark

and the woods were strangely silent and reserved, the shadows
were deepening, the earth heavy inside his bones, the earth

was made of bones, and the rabbit who would be bounding
in tomorrow's noon, strangely,

would not be him.

GIACOMETTI

the
moon
watches
Mary
buying
mittens
for
Joe
who's
gone
to
Oaxaca
with
Jane

A MOVEMENT CATCHES THE EYE

Hello, white goose beauty pain.

Bundle fire, yes, I have it.

Tree hair, yes, I have it.

The dead child fingers fast feather music under the rocks over there.

Fast mice finger sunrise face, she eats and grows tall.

Stitching a long long bluebird and canary cape.

Sit down here, I will open the bundle.

I've brought my tray of tea to the screenhouse—
damp June morning, almost too dark to read.
Down the small slope there's the garden's unfinished
cedar fence I was working on yesterday. Gateway
posts at odd heights. The dampness darkens another
degree down, then down again, air blurred with wet
wood settling its weight, slackening like a slowly
opening palm showing a small pearl, a faint *ping*
like a fallen tree seed on the tin roof, a stretching
silence and another soft *ping* the same here-not-here
fulcrummed presence as the black and yellow
gartersnake I found resting on the handsaw's flat blade
last evening when I was gathering the tools. Maybe
enjoying the sun-heated metal. Its straight-mouthed
utterly unfake face. White plated lips and obsidian
bead eyes. So real it could not be distinguished
from other things. I slid the saw out slowly
from under the snake, leaving it taut and curled
on the straw bale. Cold living flame. It only
looked at me, flickering its tongue. I too was invisible.

ELEGY

Cutting bread near the north window, a dark jot in the white
outdoors catches my eye—a dashed inkbrush line—a

fisher bounding the snow field into the far trees. It pulls
the land into itself with long grabs. Its leaps, its live tail

stretch to a black ribbon that stays in the air. I buckle on
snowshoes and follow its wide-spaced prints, intaglios

of its five toe pads and thick claws. Then drips of frozen
blood. Then stiff strands of muscle, clean as grocery-store

meat. At an elm's foot churned snow splashed
with piss. Crisscrossed tracks, more blood and piss.

When I lived near a bar, sometimes the glass smashing
and sirens would go on past dawn. From here our roof's

white ridge and smoking chimney show above the rise.

NO NAME, NO DATE

Nightfall—the clouds pull away
exposing the farm to stars and deep space.

On the dark path to the door, in slow boots, each
step we take makes the snow *squeal.*

Above, in the wooded hill—looming spiked silhouette—
something cracks like a gunshot.

Under the duvet, under the sloped roof, we sleep without
names, without age.

At dawn the frost-bent roofbeams clank and wake us.

With a pail of grain, I step onto the brittle porch in
time to see the wild turkeys gliding heavily down
from their roosts in the cottonwoods at the field's edge.

Neither wary nor oblique now, they come necks outstretched
half flying over their snow trails to the place
where I scatter feed.

In close unison, milling, they stabstabstab the fresh grain

then slacken, hunched, shifting from foot to foot, and one
by one hoist themselves with stiff huge wing-sweeps up
into the branches of the oak

where they slump, heads somewhere buried in their rumpled
heaps, sometimes drooping half-splayed fans that flash
surprising feather-glint, metallic-teal

in the level sun. Their rough brown shoulders tilt to
iridescent bronze, oiled turquoise-salmon, amber,
raspberry-gold scales. They twitch

and warm their listless dignities—old family money,
antic and darkened after millions of years.

We watch through the frost-edged window at no point
in history, feeling the same packed light.

Woodshed Hill is just beyond the window where I write.
I am alone with it for hours. It rises from underneath
the house and is not separate from the sky. It is a large
animal with a profile beautiful in all its changes. It
extends beyond where etymology can go. Old snow, all
gaps and tatters, plasters its lumpy slope. Last fall's leaves
show through the tears, and each grey oak and elm pokes
through a stretched hole. On the steep south face the snow
hangs on rocks and stumps like ripped lace. In a few months
sedge and low boughs will hide it all. Yesterday I found
the draft of a poem from March two years ago. I wrote that
the hill was "stepping out of a white distance where it had
disappeared." I said it was "moving back into its half-wrecked
home, awkward, gawky, starting again in grade nine." As though
I'd written that on the window and blocked the view. The hill is
always full-grown. It feasts when the sun comes with its followers,
but I see no end to its patience and dignity. It gathers its history
in each leaf and bone, and I have a few years living beside it,
facing it. I look up from the page to something I've never seen.

"We Make Our Long-Talked-About Trip to the One-Room School Museum": Not having crossed paths with Philip Larkin in ages, I'm surprised to see him coming out of the museum just as I'm about to go in. We nod in passing, and the door thuds shut.

"Silphium": Cyrene's precious (now extinct) silphium was not the same (also threatened) plant that Aldo Leopold writes about in the July chapter of *A Sand County Almanac*.

"Unconsoled": see Kazuo Ishiguro's *The Unconsoled*, 1995.

"In the Morning I Sit with Cézanne": *Cezanne Paintings*, Dumont Buchverlag, Cologne, 1993.

"Treo": I gathered these italicized words through research and have no speaking knowledge of them. The poem attempts to imagine an oak tree as extending out beyond the boundaries we normally assign to it, out into its physical environment and support systems; at the same time, the poem imagines the words and concepts from which the poem itself is constructed as stretching back (and out) through their etymological and cultural histories; it also tries to imagine versions of its words and concepts in the human history surrounding the tree—in the language of people who witnessed the tree before the coming of my culture and language to its location. The named, observed tree is a linguistic tree. Its roots and branches merge with its natural environment and with its human-cultural context simultaneously and indistinguishably.

ACKNOWLEDGEMENTS

Some of the poems in this collection were first published in the magazines *Arc*, *The Antigonish Review*, *Brick*, *CV2*, *Event*, *Fiddlehead*, *Halibut*, *The Malahat Review*, *The New Quarterly*, *Reliquiae* and *Riddle Fence*. My thanks to the editors of those magazines.

Early versions of "I Haven't Looked at These in Years," "Since Life Values Nothing Higher than Life," "*Treo*," "A Word Fights Speech River to Its Highest Pool," "Openings" and "A Movement Catches the Eye" first appeared in *Forty-One Pages*, published by University of Regina Press. I thank Jan Zwicky for her editorial work on that book, and Karen Clarke and everyone at University of Regina Press for their care in its publication.

I thank especially Kelly Joseph and Dionne Brand for their support and their help in creating this book.

And I thank Susan Gillis for sharing this journey.

JOHN STEFFLER is the author of six books of poetry, including *Lookout*, which was shortlisted for the Griffin Poetry Prize, *The Grey Islands* and *That Night We Were Ravenous*. His novel *The Afterlife of George Cartwright* won the Smithbooks/Books in Canada First Novel Award and the Thomas Raddall Atlantic Fiction Award. From 2006 to 2008 he was Parliamentary Poet Laureate of Canada.